T0129987

Also by Kasi Kaye Iliopoulos: *Living in Light, Love, & Truth: Change Your Life Positively*, awarded a 2015 Living Now Book Award Evergreen Bronze Medal for Spiritual Leadership. Published by Balboa Press, a Division of Hay House.

How to Create Positive Energy in Your Space is also available in e-book and iBook formats.

Audiobook

How to Create Positive Energy in Your Space is available in audio, read by the author, Kasi Kaye Iliopoulos.

Seminars, Workshops, and Meditation Sessions

How to Create Positive Energy in Your Space and *Living in Light, Love, & Truth* seminars and workshops are held periodically in Australia. The workshops explore concepts in greater detail to support you in living the life you came here to live.

Kasi Kaye Iliopoulos also facilitates events to raise the soul frequency and clear the energetic bodies of lower vibrational energies.

For further information:

http://www.quartzholistichealth.com.au
E-mail: Info@quartzholistichealth.com.au

HOW TO CREATE POSITIVE ENERGY IN YOUR SPACE

TRANSMUTE DISCORDANT ENERGY AND ACTIVATE LIGHT AND POSITIVE ENERGY IN YOUR HOME AND ENVIRONMENT

Decluttering, cleanliness, cleansing, interior design, and the use of crystals, colour therapy, plants, flowers, aroma, sound, sacred geometry, and symbology.

KASI KAYE ILIOPOULOS

BALBOA.
PRESS
A DIVISION OF HAY HOUSE

Scripture quotations marked NKJV are taken from
the New King James Version. Copyright © 1982 by
<u>Thomas Nelson, Inc</u>. Used by permission. All rights reserved.

Author of the Living Now Evergreen Book Award for Spiritual Leadership:
"Living in Light, Love & Truth"

Balboa Press books may be ordered through booksellers or by contacting:

Balboa Press
A Division of Hay House
1663 Liberty Drive
Bloomington, IN 47403
www.balboapress.com.au
1 (877) 407-4847

Print information available on the last page.

ISBN: 978-1-5043-0247-0 (sc)
ISBN: 978-1-5043-0248-7 (e)

Balboa Press rev. date: 12/19/2016

For Bonnie (BonBon). You are the most kind, courageous, beautiful, loving and loyal Soul, whose eyes only ever speak of love and wisdom. I love you with all my heart. Thank you my darling girl. God Bless You Forever.

*But whatever house you enter, first say
'Peace to this house.'*
—Luke 10:5 NKJV

*A house is built with wisdom.
And it is built up with understanding.
Storehouses are filled with perception
From all honorable and good riches.*
—Proverbs 24:3-4 NKJV

*Heaven on Earth is a choice you must make,
not a place you must find.*
— Dr Wayne W Dyer

*The spiritual virtue of a sacrament is like light;
although it passes among the impure, it is not polluted.*
—Saint Augustine

*Love begins at home, and it is not how much we do …
but how much love we put in that action.*
—Mother Teresa

*Home is where you feel at home
and are treated well.*
—Dalai Lama

Wherever you stand, be the soul of that place.
—Rumi

CONTENTS

PREFACE

The energetic imprints of your home, workplace, and vehicle have a direct connection to you. This connection influences your energy field and the energy created in your environment, which in turn influences your experience of life. It's important to learn how to neutralise lower vibrational or discordant energy so that you can activate harmony and positivity in your physical environment.

How to Create Positive Energy in Your Space explains how to assess your physical environment and its energetic imprint by looking at the land, location, and structure. You can then harmonise your environment by crystal gridding and Himalayan-salt placement to combat discord and electromagnetic smog.

How to Create Positive Energy in Your Space also explains the impact that previous residents, neighbours, and the past have had, and how to shift lower vibrational and stagnant energy by decluttering, cleanliness, cleansing, interior design, and most importantly, intent and manifestation. It also explains the use of colour therapy; chakras; plants and flowers; aroma and atmosphere; sound; sacred geometry; and symbology to activate and manifest light and positive energy in your home and space.

Your environment can then match your soul frequency, which will reduce counteracting divergent energies that are in the environment around you. This will enable you to raise your soul frequency effectively and fluently.

INTRODUCTION

Ever wonder why you felt peaceful in one home and not another? Have you experienced the feeling of being energetically drained in your work environment? What influences the energy in your physical environment? Learn how to become aware and empowered to create a physical environment that is in tune with your soul frequency.

Our physical environment carries energy imprints. Just as personal hygiene promotes a healthy immune system, our appearance promotes self-confidence, and positive thinking creates a positive life, regularly cleansing our homes, our workspaces, and even our vehicles of lower vibrational energy can greatly improve our well-being.

Here are a few examples of how the environment or space we are in, can impact us via a number of different mediums. Let's start with the sense of smell and aroma. If you are a non-smoker and you walk into a room with people smoking, you will be affected by the smoke, passively. Just because you are a non-smoker doesn't mean you are immune to the air in that room. When you walk into a room and someone has strong perfume on, just because you are not wearing the scent doesn't mean you won't be able to smell it. You will because you are in that room.

Here is another example. You can be the most strong and courageous person, but when you visit a location of a known tragedy or calamity, you will most likely be moved by distressing emotion because of the energetic imprint of the tragedy or calamity at that location. Some places like hospitals carry a lower vibrational imprint of sickness and ill-health. I know of many people who cannot bear to stay for extended periods of time in hospitals because of the lower vibrational energy that they sense.

Consider the impact that uncleanliness has. When you first enter someone else's home, you generally canvass the place and conduct an assessment, so to speak, at least subconsciously. You may notice dust on the skirting boards, dirty windows, or a messy environment—all without judgement, of course. Now take your focus back to your own home and space. Have you ever noticed the dust on the skirting boards or the cleanliness of the windows in your own home? No? That doesn't surprise me. The mind normally registers things that are changing or new, and it sets into the background those things that are mostly static and don't change often.

Apply this same logic to the energy in your environment. The energy that is static or allowed to stay will affect you. You can practice spiritual clearing and cleansing of your personal energetic field every day, but unless you also clear and cleanse your environment, it's like taking a shower and laying on a dirty and dusty floor afterward. It is inevitable that you will get dirt and dust on you. Be mindful and aware.

Spiritualists cannot effectively refine their soul frequency in an environment that does not match their soul vibration. Quite often, we overlook this aspect in our lives. We may be closed to it because our environment is outside of ourselves, and we are taught that raising our soul vibration is about what occurs inside of us. While this is true, it is also true that the energy of what is outside of us does affect our energy field and therefore our soul vibration. Being aware means that you understand this and take action to address it.

As you continue with your soul development, you will come to see that all energetic contributors affect your intuitive ability and sensitivity. If you remain in the present moment, you can create and maintain a space that is organised, clear, and cleansed. After that, you will be able to diligently focus on the clearing and cleansing of all your energetic bodies, raising your soul vibration so you can continue on your path of restoring to your original soul template and living the life you came here to live.

CHAPTER 1

Your Physical Environment and Its Energetic Imprint

Your physical environment—your home, workspace, or vehicle—holds energetic imprints from its location, structure, past residents/owners, neighbours, and past events, just to start. The energy imprint created by everything that ever occurred in an environment, both positive or negative, has an impact on the people who live there or lived there before. Liken it to places in the world where there is a rich history; people feel compelled to visit these places to first-hand experience its energy. There is a reason so many visit to feel the vibes.

When you remove clutter from your life, you also remove blocks and stagnant energy from your physical environment. This is known as *positive environmental positioning*, and it should be done with the conscious intention to clear a path so that new, clean, and crisp energy may cycle into your life. If you don't create the opportunity for this flow to happen, it won't. You must clear its path in order to reach you.

We all do so much inner work that sometimes we need to recalibrate our external environment to match our inner vibration. This supports a steady and calm flow of positive and clean energy. It is a combination of quantum electrodynamics, embedded metaphysical imprints, and our conscious intent that influences the creation and manifestation of harmonious and positive energy.

In the past, when looking for a new place to live, I always allowed my intuition to guide me in such matters. If I felt harmony and peace during the inspection, this was an indicator for me to lodge an application. I have been a successful applicant for every property, because I listened to my intuition.

Over a decade ago, as I was undergoing a transitional phase, I inspected a beautiful and quaint house that was still furnished. I asked a few questions about the previous occupant and learnt that this person was in hospital and likely to move into a nursing home. I went within and considered this. Now, none of us consciously chooses to be in an environment that will challenge us negatively, nor do we look for dense energies to centre ourselves in. What I intuited was that the previous occupant was not just ill but was close to passing (if not already passed by this time).

I considered this energetically. My intuition was confirmed by an oil-fuelled candle that was lit in the home. In many Christian Orthodox religions, a candle burning for a departed soul symbolises that the soul is eternal and omnipresent. Since I grew up in a Christian Orthodox family, I was aware of this. Now let me point out that I have no fear of recently departed souls; I know that they are one with God and transitioning and undertaking their life review. But while I loved this house, my intuition guided me to another place to live, for no other reason than the energy of the property, coupled with the transitional phase I was going through, would have made my transition more complex. Moving into that house would have introduced energy that would not have benefitted my soul development. So I thanked and informed the agent that I would not be submitting an application.

How do you manifest harmonious and positive energy in your environment? By deliberate and conscious intent and taking action to charge it clearly and positively. Unless it has been cleansed and cleared, everything physical that is around you carries with it a vibration, a past energetic imprint. It can be an ornament, a piece of jewellery, or a piece of clothing. The most powerful event that the item was associated with impacts its energy, either positively or negatively. There are a number of ways you can clear the energy in your home, workspace, or vehicle of any negative imprints or associated discordant energy that may be attached to items, and I share these techniques with you in this book.

CHAPTER 2

Land, Location, and Structure

Every piece of Mother Earth carries with it imprints of the past, as well as neighbouring energies. The land, coupled with the location and the structure upon it, can influence the energy that flows into your life.

2.1 Land

Non-indigenous people and landowners might think about land in any number of different ways—as a financial asset to increase profitability, a commodity to be bought and sold, or simply a place to live. The connection to the land for Aboriginal people, however, is unique in the world. When compared to that of non-indigenous people, their connection to the land is sacred and of spiritual significance. The land is their mother, and Aboriginal law and spirituality are intrinsically interconnected with the land. Through this connection, their culture, traditions, and sovereignty were and continue to be formed.

In Australia, the "Welcome to Country" is an important ceremony performed by Aboriginal people to help non-indigenous people recognise Aboriginal culture and history. An "Acknowledgement of Country", which is different from the "Welcome to Country" ceremony, can be performed by everyone, Indigenous or non-indigenous, to pay respect to ancestors past and present, and to the fact that one is on Aboriginal land. Australia has many sacred locations and sites across the country, and access to many of these places is prohibited to non-indigenous people without an elder's approval.

As you can appreciate, the land on which we stand, walk, build our homes, and live has a past energetic imprint that beckons to be acknowledged. Can you imagine what the natural landscape was at the location of your home before modernisation?

2.2 Location

Most of the time, our home is our haven—our sanctuary. We expect to be protected and safe from all harm within its parameters. We also spend an incredible amount of time in workplaces, second only to the time we spend in our homes. Although we may not be able to easily change the location of our homes and workplaces, we can become aware of the energy around us and what may influence us.

The first assessment is to consider the land on which you are living. Do you know what was there before your home or building was built? Was it a cleared bock of land? Was it previously an industrial or business zone? Was another dwelling there before and perhaps demolished? Consider the history of the land and previous structures to determine what energies the location you call home may express. Be sure to thank Mother Earth for the privilege of living off her land, and ask that only positive earthly energies be allowed to remain.

What surrounds your environment? Do you have a power station near you? Are power lines close to your personal space? Look around for telecommunication towers; excessive electrical energy can cause electromagnetic smog, and because it impacts our environment, it also influences our personal energy field. This smog increases the level of electrical charge of the space we occupy by flooding it with excessive positive ions. While the electrical charge of our body is small in comparison, it can increase based on our surroundings.

Our physical bodies communicate first bioelectrically and then biochemically. Our whole nervous system is signalled by positive or negative ions. The electrical events that constitute signalling in the nervous system depend upon the distribution of ions on either side of the nerve membrane. Once negative ions reach our bloodstream, they are believed to produce biochemical reactions that increase levels of the mood chemical serotonin, which helps to alleviate depression, relieve stress, and boost our life force energy. So we should make our environment plentiful in negative ions. We will explore this in greater depth later.

As I mentioned, our bodies carry their own electrical charges, and that will also impact our soul vibration. When you perform soul-healing work, your soul's vibration refines, and this allows you to access higher intelligence as you clear any discord in your mental and emotional bodies. If you have a non-invasive environment, you are able to access this intelligence much more easily. This is why many spiritualists go into nature (where negative ions are plentiful) to meditate and contemplate, as the natural environment allows for a purer connection to All-That-Is.

Complete an assessment of whether any of these highly charged items are located near your home, and we will look at ways to neutralise the negative influence as much as possible by placement of Himalayan salt lamps, a process I will explain in 2.7. Himalayan Salt to Combat Electromagnetic Smog.

Also consider what type of businesses are near you. Are they businesses that impart positivity or feel-good energy? These tend to be meeting places like churches, social clubs, sporting venues, gyms, cafes, restaurants, health-food stores, plant-produce stores, healing centres, and the like. Or are your neighbouring businesses medical clinics, hospitals, police stations, nightclubs, and law offices, which impart lower vibrational energies?

Do you live near a freeway or busy intersection? Freeways normally have a denser energy. Imagine the number of different people who are coming in close proximity to the place you call home, not to mention the pollutants coming from all those vehicles. I urge you to consider these factors when you are looking for a new home. Once again, if the surrounding areas impart positive energy, this will influence the energy in your environment, and subsequently your soul frequency and energy field.

2.3 Structure

How our homes are built can also affect energy flow, as sometimes pockets of dense energy simply don't have a clear pathway to exit out the door. Do you live in a stand-alone home or in an apartment? What is the floor plan of your home? Do you have a shared wall that divides you from your neighbours? Is it built in a way that it is easy to navigate?

Stand-alone homes provide the cleanest energy. The reason for this is that energy transference can happen through walls, and in a stand-alone home there is sufficient distance between your house and other energies (including neighbours) to act as a barrier. The closer your body and energy field are to an electrical charge—be it a person or a device—the more likely it is that its energy imprint or charge may migrate into your physical space or environment and your own energy field.

For a stand-alone home (or a unit or townhouse with definite land boundaries), there is a method you can use to protect your house and land from intruding energies, called *crystal gridding*. This technique creates a domelike barrier to any external energy intruding on your personal space.

If you live in an apartment, shared walls have the potential to let in the energy that is on the other side, depending on the type of life your wall-sharer lives and the positive ions that may emanate from the electrical appliances on the other side of the wall. The best way to deal with this is to crystal grid and Himalayan salt your apartment, in particular the shared wall.

Personally, I know that crystals have an amazing ability to shift, cleanse, and remove all negative energy. Many years ago, I was under psychic interference; I had negative energy and projections sent my way, whether it was intentional or unintentional. Being an intuitive, I could not but acknowledge this. I was making my way to a local new age store to purchase crystals, and as soon as I walked into the store, all psychic interference ceased. Instantaneously, I felt no discord. I stayed in the new age store for at least three hours appreciating the crystals and the respite from lower vibrational energies. This was my direct experience and was my confirmation of the power of crystals and the effects of higher frequencies on one's soul vibration.

I now embody a higher soul frequency further aligned to divine love, which now allows me to not experience these negative projections from external sources. While you are on this path, remember that as you progress in your life purpose and align to divine love, you will build your spiritual strength to be able to automatically and instantaneously shift and cleanse any lower vibrational energy you intuit, until such a point that you are no longer affected.

Your life will change in a positive way when you raise your soul frequency and align it to divine love. It is in this refined frequency that lower energies are no longer compatible with your soul frequency, and are therefore immobilised from causing and affecting.

In some faiths, people ask the parish priest to visit a new home and bless it. If this is available to you in your chosen faith and you feel positive about it, please do so, as this will energetically protect your home and infuse it with light and love. It is like christening a home, exactly the same way we christen our children, asking for God's anointing and protection from all harm and the guidance to live the most prosperous life possible.

You can also crystal grid your home to create positive energy. A crystal grid is an arrangement of crystals on a specific geometric shape that focuses universal life force in a particular way for a particular purpose.

The crystal to use to shield your home is black tourmaline. This is a powerful stone for protection against lower vibrational energy of all kinds, as well as a strong spiritual grounding stone. Also known as schorl, black tourmaline encourages positive attitudes, good luck, and happiness regardless of the circumstances. Black tourmaline does not absorb negative energies; instead, it cleanses, purifies, and transforms them into a higher vibration.

Black tourmaline has unique electrical and magnetic properties, so it helps ground energies to the circuit of Mother Earth's electromagnetic field. The arrangement of these crystals in a grid forms a dome or sphere like energy barrier—providing protection from electromagnetic smog and lower vibrational energies.

2.4 Cleaning, Cleansing, and Programming Crystals

Crystals have formed over eons, through shifts in the earth's plates and the activity of molten magma under the surface of the earth. All crystals have a geometrically regular shape and are built from one of seven possible geometric forms. The internal structure of a crystal is constant and unchanging. Crystals can be considered the DNA of Mother Earth, imprinted with the energy of millions of years of evolution. Crystals contain ancient and current imprints of energy.

In 2015, I took a holiday to Hawaii, mainly to attend Dr. Wayne W. Dyer's "I Am Light" seminar in Maui, which I loved. God bless his soul. I was also yearning to visit Kilauea Volcano on Big Island. I sought to be present to experience its sheer majesty.

Halema'uma'u Crater is a pit crater located within the much larger summit caldera of Kilauea. It is extraordinary. Halema'uma'u is home to Madame Pele, goddess of fire and volcanoes according to Hawaiian mythology.

I so wanted to bring home with me a piece of lava rock as a token of the amazing healing energies I experienced in Hawaii. Before you jump to conclusions, I didn't, as I learned it is said that anything natively Hawaiian—such as sand, rock, or pumice—will bring bad luck to whoever takes it away from Hawaii. Some say it is a myth and some say it was a park ranger who invented the story to deter tourists from taking lava rock and sand from Hawaii. (Hawaii also has black-, red-, and green-sand beaches that are spectacular.)

In addition, it's actually against US law to remove objects from a national park, but tourists still do. Thousands of tons of rock and sand are returned to Hawaii every year—along with apology letters declaring that the people returning the items have experienced bad luck since acquiring them.

Given that all crystals were originally created from molten magma, we are compelled to consider that they contain ancient as well as current energy imprints. We can programme crystals to a specific purpose, as I will explain in the coming pages. So if the people returning the Hawaiian sand, rock, or pumice believed the myth of Madame Pele, could they have unconsciously programmed the sand, rock, or pumice with that energy, and did that programming bring about misfortune? Or is Madame Pele's myth actually true? Whether Madame Pele's myth is true or not, it mostly comes down to respecting Mother Nature, the land, and its ancestors. It is just something to think about.

Back to preparing your crystals to use in a grid. Crystals need to be programmed to respond in the way you intend. The first step is to reset your crystals, which means that you are removing any pre-existing programmes or energies. These programmes may have come from you during a previous use, from someone else who has come into contact with them, including anyone who may have touched or admired them in the store from which you purchased them. You can cleanse and clear programmes and energies using a number of tools, including frankincense, sage, a running river, the ocean, falling rain, running tap water, earth, sound, plants, a quartz cluster, or sacred geometry. Let your intuition lead you to the method of cleansing and clearing your crystals that resonates with you.

Note: Please do not use water on soft crystals like angelite, some calcites, howlite, aragonite, azurite, dolomite, malachite, selenite, or sulphur, as it may dissolve the crystal to a greater or lesser degree.

Here are step-by-step instructions for cleansing and clearing your crystals with running tap water or falling rain (you can use captured rainwater as well):

1. Let your crystals sit in a solution of salt (three pinches) and water for a few hours and then rinse under running tap water (try not to use your kitchen sink for this). Or let your crystals sit under the falling rain for a few hours.

2. Dry your crystals either by patting them dry or placing them on a clean towel to air-dry.

3. If timing is aligned, place your crystals under the full moonlight for a night, or under the moonlight for a few nights, or in the sunlight for an hour or two to cleanse and recharge (be mindful that some crystals can fade in the sunlight).

4. Take one crystal and hold it between the palms of your hands. Visualise the crystal's energy and connect to it. Feel the crystal's energy, remembering the crystal has eons of imprints of Mother Earth.

5. With intention, clear any programmes or residual energies that are residing in the crystal until you intuitively feel it has been cleared.

6. Place an intention—such as clearing, dissolving, or transmuting lower vibrational energy and activating, multiplying, and expanding positivity, love, and light

energy—into the crystal. Say out loud what you intend for the crystal to emanate. (The process is like meditating or praying.)

7. Visualise a column of pure golden light coming down, surrounding the crystal, and sealing your energetic intentions in divine love and light.

8. Give thanks to Mother Earth and spirit.

9. Repeat Steps 4–8 process for the other crystals.

Your crystals are now ready for gridding.

2.5 Crystal Gridding Your House and Land

To grid your land, imagine a square or rectangle shape surrounding your property. Place a piece of black tourmaline (which you can bury in the richness of Mother Earth) on each corner of the land boundaries and display a larger one (as the master crystal) in the centre of your house, indoors. It doesn't matter whether the master crystal is on display in a positioned box or hanging on a ceiling mobile in the centre of your home, as long as it is located there.

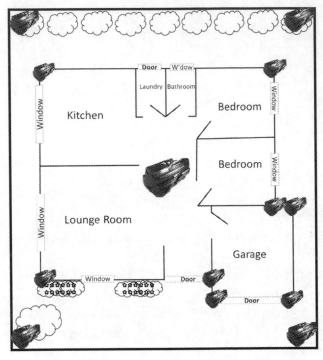

Crystal gridding your land boundaries and house
with black tourmaline

To further grid your house structure, place a piece of black tourmaline in each inside corner of your house. The internal corner placements will generate a secondary grid, connecting to each of the other crystals, creating an internal boundary against discordant energy. The centre placement creates a dome. To even further grid your house, place a smaller piece of black tourmaline indoors at the corners of each window and doorway.

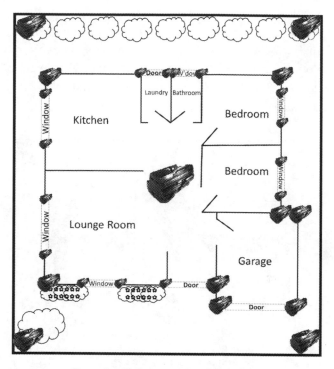

Crystal gridding your land boundary,
house, doors, and windows with black tourmaline

2.6 Sacred-Geometry Gridding

You can also use the hexagram or pentagram shape to grid your home. (To learn more about sacred geometry, refer to Chapter 12.) It helps considerably if you have a floor plan. If you don't, map your own floor plan and draw your crystal grid on the plan first. Make sure the points of the star touch or overlap the external walls of your house plan before you grid it.

Grid the points on the most external aspects of the land boundary at each of the eight points with a piece of black tourmaline (at each corner and then halfway between each land boundary corner). Place a piece of black tourmaline closest to each point in the star internally and display a larger one (the master) in the centre of your house.

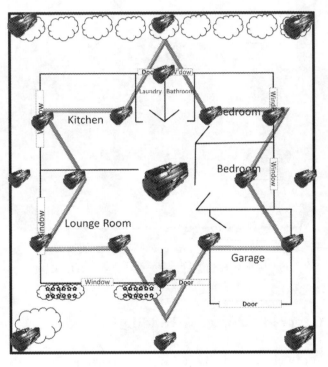

Crystal gridding using sacred geometry for your land boundary and house with black tourmaline

2.7 Crystal Gridding Your Apartment

To grid your apartment, use a square or rectangle to surround your apartment parameters. Place a piece of black tourmaline on each corner of the apartment boundaries (all corners in the parameter of your apartment, if it is not square or rectangular) and display a larger one (as the master) in the inside centre of your apartment. To further grid your apartment regarding neighbourly energies, place a piece of black tourmaline internally at each corner of each room of your apartment, on all shared walls.

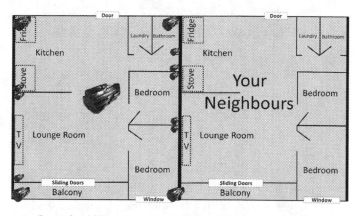

Crystal gridding your apartment with black tourmaline
(boundary and shared wall)

Also consider placing selenite crystals on the shared walls between the black tourmaline corner placements in each room. This will strengthen the gridline, as selenite magnifies the energies of black tourmaline, connecting to each of the other crystals and creating an impervious boundary against discordant energy that might otherwise filter through the shared wall. The centre placement creates a dome. To further grid your apartment, place a smaller piece of black tourmaline indoors at the end of each window and doorway.

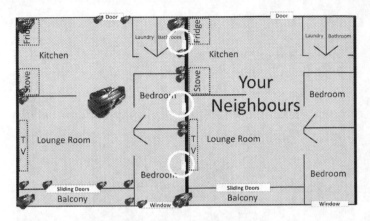

Crystal gridding your apartment with black tourmaline and selenite (boundary, shared wall, entry, and windows)

I suggest that if you decide to crystal grid your home or apartment that you buy an additional set of black tourmaline and/or selenite crystals. While black tourmaline does not need to be cleansed as often as other crystals (as it does not store discordant energies), it helps to cleanse and recharge the crystals every so often. Just follow the cleaning, cleansing, and programming instructions from Section 2.4—with the exception that selenite crystals can erode in water so it is best to smudge them to clear out residual energy and programmes.

If you want to keep your grid in place, then as you remove the ones to be cleansed, replace them with extra crystals that have already been cleansed, recharged, and programmed. Once you have replaced the crystals with the cleansed ones, charge and reprogram the used ones, setting the intention of protection of your home and land.

The crystals can be hung on the wall or placed on the floor in the indicated positions. Be creative in your display of crystals. If you live in a multi-story home, repeat the placement on the other floors as well.

2.8 Himalayan Salt to Combat Electromagnetic Smog

We spoke about electromagnetic smog earlier—it's produced by high-voltage items and electrical appliances, including power lines, refrigerators, washing machines, and microwave ovens—and how Himalayan salt may help in these situations. I will first say that the best form of clearing electromagnetic smog is fresh, breezy air, so open your windows when you can and let clean air into your home. In place of that, Himalayan salt lamps work well.

Himalayan salt is around 250 million years old and comes from a large salt lake that naturally dried. It lies under the earth's surface because of geological shifts, and so it has been protected from pollution, contamination, and man-made interference. It is mined from underground salt caves. No single man-made laboratory-created product or any other salt has as many of the ninety-two trace minerals known to man, in their naturally occurring state and in the same proportion as the human body, as Himalayan salt does. You can even use it in place of your white salt in the kitchen.

Himalayan salt lamps in particular have been scientifically shown to increase negative ion presence—in effect neutralising excessive positive ions that may be present in your environment. Place the salt lamps near electrical appliances like fridges, televisions, and computers. The negative ions that Himalayan salt lamps emit kill bacteria, purify the air, reduce radiation, increase well-being, and soothe the mind, body, and soul. Negative ions are found naturally in nature during thunderstorms, at waterfalls, at the beach, in rainforests, and wherever nature is most pure.

A heated Himalayan salt lamp will attract water molecules (moisture) from the air, forming a solution of NaCl (sodium chloride) and H_2O (water). Sodium is a positive ion and chloride a negative ion. The evaporation of water through salt emits negative ions, which is how Himalayan salt lamps work. You can use Himalayan salt tea-light holders for the same purpose.

When living in an apartment with shared walls, you should not only assess where your electrical appliances are positioned but also where electrical appliances may be positioned in your neighbours' apartments on a shared wall. Your bedroom walls may be shared with your neighbour's lounge room walls, and almost always there will be a television located on the other side. Most people do not turn their appliances off at the switch (when you do, you limit the emitting of positive ions), so there will be a positive electrical charge present almost all the time. If the head of your bed sits flush to this wall, then as you sleep, you will be inundated with positive ions, which won't make you feel good. They will affect your rest time and may make you feel lethargic.

I strongly suggest placing a Himalayan salt lamp on your bedside table on this shared wall. Leave it on as much as possible—at least for some time before you retire for the day. Place one at any point on the shared wall where there is likely to be an electrical appliance in your neighbour's apartment. This will produce negative ions to counteract the positive ones on the other side of the wall.

Next, do an assessment of your house or apartment. Where are your electrical appliances? Do you switch appliances off from the wall switch when not in use (except for the refrigerator, of course)? If not, I suggest you develop a habit of doing so. Not only will you save on electricity consumption, you will reduce the emitting of positive ions.

Also assess where other electrical charges may be coming from and strategically place Himalayan salt lamps or Himalayan salt tea-light holders in your house or apartment as appropriate. Again, be creative when completing the placement. Himalayan salt lamps are a beautiful feature, so make the most of them.

Congratulations! You have prepared your physical environment to minimise electromagnetic smog and discordant energy that may otherwise, migrate into your personal space.

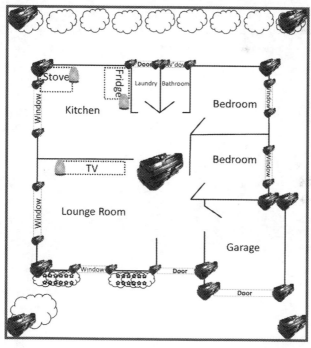

Crystal gridding your land boundary, house, doors, and windows with black tourmaline, plus Himalayan salt lamp placement for electromagnetic smog reduction

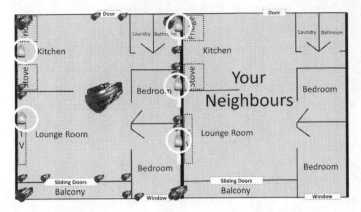

Crystal gridding your apartment with black
tourmaline and selenite (boundary, shared wall,
entry, and windows), plus Himalayan salt lamp
placement for electromagnetic smog reduction

CHAPTER 3

Previous Residents, Neighbours, and the Past

If you live in a pre-existing property, there will always be an energetic imprint present from the previous residents. If they didn't clear the energy in the space when they left, it is up to you to do the clearing so you can activate the space with clean, positive energy.

For example, if the previous residents had financial difficulty in their life, it is likely that this energy is still present. It is not uncommon for people to move house and then say, "Since we moved here, everything has been a disaster." This negative impact on people's lives tends to occur because of the remaining lower vibrational energy in the home they have moved in to. They may even say the place is bad luck, or that they feel they have been cursed somehow. But it is not that at all. It is simply negative energy that is lingering, and the good news is that it can be cleansed and cleared and removed from the place and space you call home. There is no spooky connotation to this. It is physics, and it is intent and intuition that do the clearing and cleansing.

Most of us rely on our five physical senses to explain phenomena, like sight, smell, taste, sound, and touch—and we often exclude our intuitive feelings. Please don't wind yourself up if you are in this circumstance. Feel and connect to your positive intention to clear away any and all discordant energy. Later in this chapter, I will share with you a clearing manifestation to cleanse and evoke positive vibrations in your home.

Neighbours and their way of life impact the energy of our homes and workplaces. You spend a lot of time in your home, and if you have neighbours who live disconnected lives, how do you think that will impact you? For example, if they are frequent drug users or consume excessive alcohol, or even if they have moderate narcissistic traits, the energy associated with them can invade your personal space whether you like it or not. By using your sense of feeling and intuition, you can cleanse your space and place a light-filled barrier by which such discordant energy is repelled.

Even if you're not friends with your neighbours, their energy is close enough to a place you call home—your abode, your haven, your sanctuary—that it may affect you. That works out well if your neighbours live a life of light and love; you would be uplifted in your living situation because of the positive energy radiating from them. In this circumstance, however, I caution you to make sure you are not an unconscious energy-taker. Create and manifest your own positive energy because no one appreciates takers of positive energy; they are sometimes referred to as psychic vampires. Receiving energy that is given is different from taking energy that is not. Different universal laws apply.

The same applies anytime you are in the same room as a positive person. You will most likely be uplifted, but be sure to contribute positive energy yourself. Don't fall into a victim mentality and take this energy; don't be jealous and try to break this energy; and don't get resentful and try to compete with this energy. If your response is not one of light and love, you are creating negative karma for yourself. I suggest you don't do it. Instead, be responsible for the energy that you emanate via thought, words, actions, feelings, emotions, and perceptions.

Just because a number of people fail to take responsibility for the energy they emanate doesn't mean that you should do the same. If someone is not responsible with the energy they emanate, that is a lesson they will learn in their life journey. The cycle of negativity will occur in their life until they choose otherwise. Don't think, "They are not being energetically responsible, so why should I?" What you emanate out into the universe circles back to you, so keep it positive.

We all know of places that have had a tragic event happen. If we visit the site of a tragic event, we will likely be moved by emotions like sorrow, compassion, and empathy. For example, when I visited Auschwitz and Birkenau in Poland in 2009, the energy of the camps was heavy, sad, and dense. Simply by being completely aware of the past at this location, I was able to acknowledge what I was intensely feeling. The horrendous events that occurred at Auschwitz, are imprinted at that location, although they happened some seventy-five years ago. I could feel the fear and how souls young and old were deprived of their divine rights. The feeling is of complete desolation. I cried during my visit there and for days after. Tears are rolling down my face as I am writing this because those imprints are a frequency I will never forget, as it altered my life and the work I do today. Be mindful, you will feel the imprint of energy at a location wherever you are, and whether you are consciously aware of it or not.

The same applies to you and the location you are in. These places carry an energetic imprint of events—which is why, when people visit these sites, the intuitive self feels it. If you do not know that a tragic event occurred and don't practice clearing and activating a grid of protection, you will feel it; the difference is, the intellectual mind has no knowledge of the event, so you feel out of sorts. You tend not to attribute it to the past energy imprint and perhaps just conclude that you are not feeling the best at that point in time. You might even mistake it as intuition that something bad has happened or is going to happen. While this is most often not the case, if you are connected to your higher self, it will show you the reason for the discord.

The same can be said of the past residents and past events of your home, even if the event happened years ago. When discordant energies are allowed to stay in your environment, they will. But you can clear, cleanse, and transcend this discordant energy.

How do you do this? By intent and manifestation. Remember, the energy we embody will anchor and attract a like energy into our lives. Even if the energy was not created by us in the first place, like if someone projects or intends discordant energy toward you and you accept it as your own and allow it to stay, it will. If your intent is positivity, peace, and abundance, that's what will manifest in your life. Intent is about activating your actions, words, thoughts, feelings, and emotions with the outlook of positivity, peace, and abundance—and then manifesting it because you have embodied the energy frequency of what it feels like as if it is so. Then it will be so.

When clearing and cleansing energy, spiritualists frequently use incense or an energy room spray. I explain more about these tools later in the book. You can also work with God; Jesus; ascended masters; the divine legions of light; deities; saints and archangels; source; and All-That-Is. The determining factor is what resonates with you and your soul energy, and most importantly where you are in your soul journey.

As a suggestion, here is a meditation you can use to clear any discordant energies from your home:

> *I ask for all expressions of negativity, fear, anger, anxiety, and interference from all planes of existence, from the past, from past residents, and from past events, and any and all discordant energy transfer from my neighbours from all cardinal sides [and above and below, if you are an apartment] to be sent to All-That-Is, to be transmuted to the highest form of light possible and gifted to Mother Earth—and in turn, to be replaced with pure divine and positive energy. I clearly see the sphere of positivity and protection surrounding my home. It is done.*

Once you set this intent, believe it. I will also strongly point out that if you use intent and manifestation, whatever you are intending or manifesting will remain connected to your soul and life. If it is love and light, that's what will be attracted to your soul and life. We are affected by the energy we create. This is the karmic cycle and the universal law of energetic responsibility.

CHAPTER 4

Decluttering to Remove Blocks

Decluttering removes the energetic maze and blocks in your physical environment. Is it easy to navigate in your personal space—from floor plan to desk plan? Do you know where everything is? Have you sorted through what you need to keep and what you can donate or dispose of from your environment? Do you keep it, sell it, donate it, or dispose of it?

When we declutter or sort through our space, it is a great opportunity to get organised or pay it forward—meaning, can anything that is in your possession that is no longer needed or required, help someone else? You can help the collective consciousness by passing on what is no longer required in your life and create positive karma in your own life.

The same energy imprint takes place when you make donations. Donating items to free up your own space says that while the object is no longer is required in your life, you will allow another soul to benefit from it. This opens the door and allows other useful and more-suitable energy to enter your environment as well as, again, creating positive karma in your life.

When you donate goods, it is important that you ask for all your soul energy that is associated with the item to be returned to you. Calling back your energy is your God-given right. It basically is a consolidation and recalibration of your soul power—your battery pack. How do you do this? Easy. Just say the following or something along these lines:

> *With this item, I cleanse, purify, and call back all my soul energy, fragments, and essences into my energy field. I ask that any negative imprints be released to the universe to be transmuted into the highest form of light possible and gifted to Mother Earth. My connection to this item is completed. I welcome the new owner to enjoy and experience positivity in association with this cleansed item. It is done.*

You can also call God; Jesus; ascended masters; the divine legions of light; deities; saints and archangels; source; and All-That-Is forth, to help you.

By cleansing the items of negative imprints, you are removing any discordant energy that will be transmuted by the divine powers that be. This cleansed energy will be gifted to Mother Earth. It will transform any negativity into positivity and then ground the cleansed energy to the matrix of Mother Earth.

Do this also for items that you acquire second-hand, whether furniture or clothing. As the new owner, you can say something like this:

> *With this item, I ask that any negative imprints be released to the universe to be transmuted into the highest form of light possible and gifted to Mother Earth. I will enjoy and experience positivity in association with this cleansed item, with no remnants from its past remaining. It is done.*

We often hear about the term *non-attachment* and the importance of not forming any attachment to physical possessions. As Lao Tzu said in the Tao Te Ching, *"To understand the limitation of things, desire them."* Meaning, if we are attached to things, we are limited, and the way to become limitless is to become unattached to things. While this is true and the healthiest way to live, it is not always emotionally possible. We all have possessions that hold sentimental value. When you keep such things as your children's first booties or photos of your children as babies or a plane ticket from your most favourite overseas trip or even your wedding ring, these are really positive items to keep in your environment. They have a positive energetic association to them and thus draw like energy into the environment surrounding you.

Here is an example of what Lao Tzu is referring to. If you have an attachment to your wedding ring, you will only feel you are married when you wear the ring on your left ring finger. You know you are married, but it is the emotional attachment to a physical thing that influences what you feel. If you feel funny or bare when you take off your wedding ring, this is exactly what Lao Tzu is referring to. If you desire or need a thing in order to feel, then you become limited. The reality is, you are married, full stop, whether or not you are wearing your wedding ring.

For other items, if you intuitively feel you want to keep certain items because they have a significant meaning to you, then please do. Your focus when decluttering is to sort through what you can donate or dispose of—items that you don't have a genuine need for. Pay special attention to items that carry with them negative and disruptive energy because of their association with your past; items that are no longer usable; or items you really have no need for.

For example, if you have a treadmill that you have not used in two years, you may know, intuitively, that you will not be using it in the next two years, as you have no intention of doing so. Or you may be constantly saying, "I have to start using the treadmill again." All this information is important and will indicate what action you should take. If you have no intention of using the treadmill and it is not your thing, sell or donate it—once it is cleared of your energy—so someone else can enjoy it. If you sell it, then you benefit from the financial aspect; it is like transcending that possession into financial energy to put toward something that will return positive and active energy. If you have an intention of using the treadmill soon, then dear soul, put it on your to-do list sooner rather than later. Set the intention to utilise your item and the associated energy of it to bring about positive and active energy in your life.

If you have an intention to use the treadmill and don't, you create an energy block. You are saying, "I want to use the treadmill and exercise but I am not," so you harbour stagnant energy. When you donate the treadmill, you are clearing and making room for something new and creating positive karma. When you sell it, you are utilising the energy to activate positivity and flowing financial energy elsewhere in your life.

If you are not accustomed to selling or disposing of goods, you can segregate them for a certain period of time. If you have not used the item after a set period of time—say, six months—then you can deem that you have no use for it. Then sell it or donate it.

Keep in mind that when you rearrange your physical items, like personal belongings and furniture, this will shift the energy in that space and in your home, so if you have a feeling that such a shift of energy is taking place, acknowledge that this is what has likely happened. Try to complete the process detailed in the next chapter, "Cleanliness to Promote Clean Energy," as soon as you can after you have decluttered your environment.

CHAPTER 5

Cleanliness to Promote Clean Energy

The cleanliness of your environment is of great importance. If your environment is clean, it welcomes clean, fresh energy into your home or workplace. Remember that like energy is attracted to your personal spaces; if your personal spaces are not clean, then you can expect unclean energy to be attracted.

When you do a total cleaning of your home, how good does it feel that your home is super clean? That feeling when you retire into bed for the evening and you look around at your days' work and feel really good—that is clean energy attracting clean energy.

So where do you start? Start with one room and then work your way around your home. Clean your windows and corners of cobwebs, dust your windowsills and skirting boards, wipe scuff marks off walls, and so on. I suggest that you don't use any chemical cleaners; instead, choose either plant-based cleaners, hot water and detergent, vinegar, or bicarbonate of soda. This reduces the pollutants in your environment and is much healthier for you. If you choose to go chemical-free, you can still maintain the cleanliness of your home by cleaning on a more frequent basis. I suggest you consider this, especially if children and animals share your living space.

Try to declutter and clean your home over the span of one whole day, and if that's not possible, over the course of successive days. If it is a family home, task your family with duties in their rooms to achieve this. When you finish cleaning your home, you will then be ready to cleanse and clear discordant and lower vibrational energies.

CHAPTER 6

Cleansing to Clear Discordant Energy

Cleansing means to clear any stagnant, discordant energy and to move it up and out of your environment. If a negative energy imprint has been allowed to embed itself into your environment or possessions, it is your job to say, "Hey, there is the exit. Off you go. In love and light."

It is much like airing out an expensive dry-clean-only garment that has been hanging in your wardrobe for years. While it is expensive and most likely a beautiful garment, you would still air it out to remove the embedded stale air, yes? That is what cleansing your environment is about. You have uncluttered your home, and you have either kept, sold, donated, or disposed of items. You have cleaned your home top to bottom, and also the items you have kept. Now you need to cleanse the energy in it.

Note that when you declutter and clean your home, any discordant energy that was stagnant is likely to have shifted within your environment, so now you shift it out of your environment. Again, intent and manifestation. You can say something along the lines of:

I ask that all expressions of discord, negativity, fear, anger, anxiety, and interference are cancelled and deleted on all planes of existence, from the past, in the present, including parallel and future dimensions. I infuse all the floors, walls and ceilings, and everything in my home, with love and light; and I allow only that which is love and light to affect me, my energy field, my home, my family and my life. I clearly see the sphere of positivity and protection. It is done.

You should immediately feel the room becoming lighter. I suggest you move from room to room and set the intent to cleanse any remnants of discord. And when you do, know and feel that it has been done. You can do this exercise at any time when you feel your home needs a boost of positive energy.

CHAPTER 7

Interior Design to Improve Flow

The interior design of our environment involves the selection and arrangement of ornaments, display items, and furniture. It is to engage the five senses to see, hear, taste, smell, and touch in order to feel intuitively (our sixth sense). Feelings or intuition can be triggered by our environment via the five senses, so be mindful and be present in what you choose to display in your internal environment.

7.1 Entrance

Key themes: love, safe home, harmony

The entrance to your home should make you say "Home, sweet home." Your home should be a place of prosperity on all levels. Many people place two jade plants at the entrance of their home. According to feng shui, these represent prosperity and wealth, and it is a bonus that they are easy to care for, being succulent plants.

Let your entrance be the place where you take a deep breath and are grateful to be home. Place items like crystals, especially citrine (the crystal of abundance and sunshine), in your entrance. Add favourite photos that embody happy and peaceful moments in your life and your family's life.

Do you have a life to-do list of the places you want to visit and the things you wish to achieve? If you do, this is a perfect place to keep it. Place it on display without a glass pane or protective cover; if you place it in a frame, remove the glass so that you can tick off and date each aspiration as you achieve it.

Every day, you will see your life to-do list, and you will remember it. If you remember it, you will actively embody the intent of doing it. If you embody the intent, you will embody the feeling, and it will manifest in your life.

7.2 Lounge Room

Key themes: peace and intellect

The lounge room tends to be one the most frequented spaces in your home (while you are awake). Make it a relaxing and insightful area, where your intuition is free and your intellect active.

In this space, we entertain or watch movies to relax or learn. It is the hub of family time and connection. You may also read a book in this space, so it should be relaxing and a learning centre while you are awake and aware in the physical.

If you have some favourite books, place them on your coffee table. If you have favourite photos, place them on display.

Most importantly, this room should be the extension of your entrance in terms of feeling and ambience. It should positively welcome you through the front door into your abode, every single day.

7.3 Bedroom

Key themes: protection, rejuvenation, and recalibration

Your bedroom is the room you spend the most time in, and it is also the room where you are mostly not physically awake. A lot of your own healing happens while you sleep because the mind—the ego—does not have conscience thoughts to control.

Therefore, your bedroom should be a haven that allows your mind, body, and soul to rejuvenate and recalibrate while in a theta state. Make your bedroom clean, calming, and positive. Look around. What do you see that perhaps doesn't belong in the bedroom? How organised is the room? Do you store dirty laundry here? What condition is your bedding in? Is it tattered and worn? When was the last time you replaced your pillows with new ones? When is the last time you washed your quilt or blankets? I ask the questions of you for the sheer fact that energy will embed in your items. So how energetically clean are these items really?

These questions are important to determine whether your bedroom promotes positive energy, as your soul will soak it up as you sleep. To make this room the most tranquil space in the house, display photos that make you smile and give you gratitude for life—ornaments that make you feel good, paintings or wall hangings that you just love and that radiate light. Your bedroom says a lot about how you define yourself, how you appreciate yourself, and how much self-love you have.

Your bedroom should not be a place of worry and anxiety. You may have used this space to unintentionally magnify energy—through fear and worry, for example—because it is often a space of your very own, especially if you live with other people.

Lay on your bed and relax. Now pay specific attention to where your mind wanders. Are you in the habit of worrying about life, or are you in the habit of thinking about how good life is? Do your thoughts shift from the present moment to memories of the past or anxiety about the future? Intent, intent, intent, dear souls! Be ever so mindful. Evoke a feeling of gratitude and a knowing of protection, and practice it continuously until it is constant.

Have you ever wondered why, in so many hotels, the Holy Bible can be found in the bedside table drawer? It has the spiritual significance of protection, and you would probably be surprised how many people have one in their bedside table drawer at home. Once again, it is the intent. If the Bible is not your thing, perhaps leave your favourite inspiring book on your bedside table and read a few lines each morning and night to embody the feeling of protection, trust, and gratitude in all life.

7.4 Kitchen

Key theme: nourishment, perfect health, and wellness

Your kitchen should represent how you nourish your physical body and subsequently your mind and soul. Keep all your food stores fresh and in-date. Consider the water you drink and perhaps make space for a filtered dispenser or spring water.

You have heard the expression, "Your body is your temple." Well, the food that you consume should be representative of this sacred temple of yours that houses your soul. Place your favourite fresh fruit in a bowl on your kitchen table or bench so that when you spot it, you think, "Mmmm." Cook a homemade meal and allow the aroma to be present in your kitchen, so that when you smell it, you again think, "Mmmm." Why do I suggest this? We often fail to acknowledge our senses in our homes and day-to-day lives, and all senses impact our energy field.

Think back to when, perhaps, your mum or grandma, or your dad or grandpa, cooked a signature meal. You could smell it as soon as you walked in, and you couldn't wait to sit at the table to eat—that is, if you didn't take a portion and nibble at it before you even sat at the table. The fact that you recall the smell and feeling should be enough for you to realise that smell and sight activate feelings via past imprints that we store in our energy field. Evoke past positive imprints that are activated by your senses in the present moment, as they impact your energy field and the future.

7.5 Bathroom

Key theme: cleansed and purified

Your bathroom is where you physically cleanse your entire body, and the room should represent this. Sometimes a toilet is located in the bathroom, so make sure that the toilet is cleaned frequently. It is where waste leaves your home, so make sure you allow for energetic waste to follow suit.

Your bathroom is also the place where you clean your body—your temple. When you shower, also clean your shower. If you walk into a shower with a dirty body and then walk out clean, the dirt is still in the shower. That dirt includes dirty energy that may have been clinging to your energy field. Get rid of that dirty energy. It is easily done by cleaning the shower while you are in it. Everything has an impact on your energy field, so keep everything super clean when you can.

7.6 Office

Key theme: organised, in order, and perfect wealth

Your office is where you get your finances in order—bills, insurance, taxes, etc. Your office may even be where you conduct a lot of your research about life. It is where you determine your budget and financial spending. Keep this space organised and neat. Know where everything is; file it in folders or a filing system. If you don't have a diary, consider buying one to keep on top of bills and payments as they become due. Or use the electronic diary on your computer or mobile device.

The energy from this room will impact your financial status and the order in your life. If you are experiencing financial hardship, place specific focus on this room and follow the decluttering, cleaning, and cleansing process to improve your financial status and put your life in order. Try it and test it, and observe the improvements.

7.7 Meditation Room/Sacred Space

Key theme: inspiration and divine connection

Your meditation room or sacred space in your home should best represent your soul—the spiritual aspect of yourself. It represents your dreams and desires, and your positivity in thought and feeling. It is where you activate your soul's creativity in vision and then manifest it into your physical life. It is your place of divine peace and serenity.

Let this be an area that embodies clear, magical, and positive intention. You can decorate the area with whatever has divine significance to you, or you can keep it clean and minimalised. Whatever your intuition guides you to do will be the right thing for you.

Many spiritualists work with ascended masters, divine beings, and the legions of light, and they fill their meditation space with items of significance that include pictures or statues of Buddha, Archangel Michael, Mother Mary and Jesus Christ, or items of symbolic reference like crosses, peace signs, or "om" signs. The sacred and symbolic significance of these physical items transcends to the etheric planes and into energetic levels in the space in which they are in. It is totally up to you what you choose, if anything, to display.

Crystals are also wonderful to place in your sacred space. Rose quartz, for example, will emit divine love in your space.

Also, if you have a vision board, this is the perfect place to display it. Vision boards are collages of pictures, tokens, and symbols that are brought to life through your vision and creativity. A vision board can be as big or as small as you wish. It is a visualisation of what you wish to manifest in your life through the sense of sight, which transpires into feeling.

Keep your sacred space extremely clean. Clean it at least every couple of days. You may opt to burn a white candle and incense to purify the area afterward as well. Most importantly, this area should also be cleansed and protected with an energetic field—or sacred circle, as many know it—via intent and the spoken word. You might say something like this:

> *I ask that any and all negative, discordant, fear-based, interfering, and intrusive energies are cancelled and deleted. From the north, south, west, and east, and from above and below, I surround this space with golden white light, only allowing entrance to that which is of love and light, and for my highest good. I am protected. It is done.*

This is a very basic intention, and you can add to or personalise it in any way you wish. You can also call God; Jesus; ascended masters; the divine legions of light; deities; saints and archangels; source; and All-That-Is forth, to help you. You can ask that each of the cardinal archangels surround your sacred space as well. This is totally up to you, and you can also call for the energy of saints you work with, if any. It is just important to set and activate the higher intention of love, purity, and protection, especially before you start your prayer, meditation, or manifestation activities.

This space is where you open your chakras, including your crown chakra, and connect and allow two-way flow to the divine source. Make sure your sacred space is complimentary to that. Because you are working from your soul space, you open a connection to the divine through you.

7.8 Outdoor Area

Key theme: nature and grounded

Your outdoor area should be a place of nature and connection to Mother Earth. Don't worry too much if you only have a balcony; you can still achieve this connection.

Place grounding items like rocks, potted plants, grass, fountains, or wind chimes in this area. The flora and fountains will produce the negative ions that we spoke about earlier, which will make you feel great. Include an outdoor seat so you can sit and read a book, meditate, or just relax. Let yourself enjoy this space, and if you have the opportunity to once in a while, settle your feet into the earth when you feel you are ungrounded. This will send your soul energy and base chakra cords into the ground and to the core of Mother Earth, helping you ground, rebalance, and recalibrate with pure and positive Mother Earth energies. If you have dogs or cats, make sure that it is a wonderful, safe, and relaxing place for them too.

CHAPTER 8

Colour Therapy

Colour can affect moods and emotions and even how one thinks. Colour is prevalent in retail stores to influence consumer behaviour, and colour plays a major part in advertising. Architects take care when determining the colours used on structures. The interior of our homes are subject to many test-paint patches until we feel the colour is right. If you can relate to any of these actions, you already use colour as therapy.

More specifically, colour therapy involves using the seven colours of the spectrum (violet, indigo, blue, green, yellow, orange, and red) to stimulate the body's own healing process while rejuvenating and balancing energy centres known as chakras.

Each of the seven colours of the spectrum corresponds to one of the seven main chakras. When one of these chakras is experiencing difficulty, displaying the appropriate colour in your environment can cleanse and rebalance chakra energy to operate at optimum frequency. In addition, each of these chakras connects to your physical anatomy, emotions, feelings, and thoughts.

Colour therapy treats our physical, emotional, mental, and spiritual bodies and environments. It may involve exposure to coloured lights, visualising of vibrant colours, wearing of coloured clothing, eating of naturally coloured foods, and more. Colour therapy is almost always utilised in homes or workspaces.

Colour activates our emotional and mental bodies (past and present) via sight. We associate with colours through everyday life, and they do affect our thoughts and feelings. There is an ongoing debate as to whether white and black are colours or not; this depends on whether they are pigment (tone) or light-generated (colour). In the context of colour therapy, we will refer to them as colours.

White is strongly associated with new beginnings and peace. It is the dominant colour of weddings and newborn souls. At the opposite end, black is dominant at funerals. What would you think and feel if a bride wore a black wedding dress? Be honest—would it seem out of place and unusual? What if the mourners at a funeral of a passed-over soul, were all dressed in vibrant colours without the request of the passed soul? Would you think and feel differently? We have a predetermined response to colour via sight, normally created by our conditioning in society, which then associates to experiences, and activates our memories and emotions.

Colours can relate to any object, including walls and ornaments. Colour therapy is strongly related to crystal therapy, and as such crystals can be placed in your environment, as I cover in the chakra explanations below. The colours that are related to the chakra system are as follows:

1. *Red:* base chakra
2. *Orange:* sacral chakra
3. *Yellow:* solar plexus chakra

4. *Green/pink*: heart chakra
5. *Blue*: throat chakra
6. *Indigo*: third eye/brow chakra
7. *Violet*: crown chakra (gold and white are often substituted here)

I have also included the lotus flower that relates to each of the main chakras.

The Chakra System

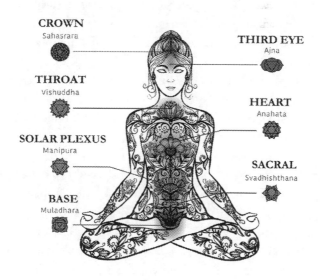

Next time you feel like painting your walls yellow or purchasing a bouquet of yellow flowers, ask yourself why. What healing energy is your intuition wanting to magnify in your home and within you? We can learn a lot about ourselves, homes and work environment by just looking around and identifying which colours we are choosing to decorate our spaces.

Colour therapy can be used to heal negative aspects of the relating chakra or to magnify positive aspects. Use colour therapy any way that is comfortable for you. However the colour is visualised—whether you paint a feature wall, display specific crystals in your home, have flowers or plants around your home, eat naturally coloured foods, or select a coloured lampshade in your lounge room—it will still have the same healing effect to help you relate to the chakra and return or energise it to a state of harmony.

When you are feeling out of balance for whatever reason, wear whatever colour you need for that day. You may also choose to incorporate colour therapy via your sleepwear or underwear. You may even decide to purchase a throw rug in a specific colour. Some souls also use colour in a healing blanket or shawl.

Note that intent is important. Colour therapy independently will help energetically with chakra openings and cleansing, but when it is used with the intent of our higher selves, it intensifies.

Below are detailed insights into each colour and its connection to the chakras, related body parts, its energetic imprint, and how it may impact your energy fields and environments. You can gain some insight as to where your intuition subconsciously has brought about colour-therapy healing energy around you and your physical environment. These insights are presented in two aspects; 'When in harmony' (which is the full embodiment of the soul in this physical life), and, 'When out of harmony' (which is minimal or no embodiment of the soul in this physical life) –that describe each colour and chakra. Please keep in mind that you may be anywhere in between these two aspects, and you will move back and forth as you continue on your path of enlightenment and apply the knowledge gained from lessons in your life.

8.1 Colour Focus: Red

Red relates to the base or root chakra. Its centre is located at the base of the spine in the coccygeal region. It links the Soul with the physical world.

This chakra governs the fight-or-flight response when survival is under actual or perceived threat. Physically, it governs sexuality; emotionally, it governs sensuality; mentally, it governs stability; and spiritually, it governs the sense of security of self and life. The base chakra is the foundation of evolving and acceptance of self as a soul in a physical body.

Related body parts: dense and solid parts of the body—bones, teeth, nails, legs, and arms—and the lower organs of the digestive/reproductive system.

Related gems/crystals: ruby, smoky quartz, garnet, agate, and bloodstone.

When in harmony, you sense a profound connection to nature and trust in universal laws, with a deep understanding of life's ebb and flow. Material abundance is recognised as secondary to a purposeful life. Red promotes the ability to remain calm in stressful situations.

When out of harmony, you are unable to trust nature and focus only on material possessions. There is a need to satisfy your own desires and wishes, and a tendency to worry excessively about any unknown outcome. Jealousy and competition are dominant emotions, as you experience life in duality instead of unity. Acceptance of self has not occurred, so acceptance of other souls has also not occurred. If any of these elements relate to you, red is your healing colour.

Base Chakra
Colour: Red
4 Petaled Lotus

8.2 Colour Focus: Orange

Orange relates to the sacral chakra (also called the navel chakra) located in the abdomen, its centre located slightly below the belly button. It is the centre for sexual energy, creativity, desire, and pure emotions. It is this area that holds our centre of gravity, helping us to define our place in the world and where we find our power to transfer thought into action.

Emotionally, the sacral chakra governs intimacy and allows feelings and emotions to flow freely, strengthening relationships. Mentally, it governs the balance of friendship in relationships, and spiritually, it balances the free giving and receiving of true feelings and emotions.

Related body parts: the reproductive system, kidneys, bladder, pelvic area, and all the liquids and fluids of the body.

Related crystals: moonstone, carnelian, and orange calcite.

When in harmony, you feel considerate, open, friendly, and kind, with no trouble sharing emotions and feelings with others. You have the ability to creatively work out a situation to get to the core of the issue and resolve it, feeling happily connected to life.

When out of harmony, you feel a lack of sureness and stability in sexual and emotional matters and an inability to express feelings, as well as a suppression of your natural and inner needs. There is a lack of boundaries and a heaviness caused by energy that is not calm, flowing, or balanced. If the sacral chakra is closed, there is tendency for isolation, a lack of nurturing ability, and a feeling of being disconnected from the universe. If any of these elements relate to you, orange is your healing colour.

Sacral Chakra
Colour: Orange
6 Petaled Lotus

8.3 Colour Focus: Yellow

Yellow relates to the solar plexus chakra located just below the ribs. The position in the centre of the body gives this chakra its significance and relates to power, will, intellect, and judgement. When you start on your spiritual journey, the solar plexus tends to be the area most affected physically because this, metaphorically, is your own personal sun. It wants to amplify your light.

This chakra is the centre for desires and wishes to blend with insight and guidance coming from universal forces above. It is concerned with the area of your personality, how you feel about yourself, and what perception you have of others. Feeling and being are integrated here; emotional energies flow externally and are understood, but not created, by the mind. This is the connection centre of spiritual and earthly aspects.

Physically, the solar plexus chakra governs the mental self as it helps awaken an enthusiasm for life along with greater confidence and optimism. It governs mental activity; openness to learning and utilising acquired knowledge, concentration, and focus; and happiness. It also dissipates fear. Spiritually, yellow is related to the your own evaluation of self holistically.

Related body parts: digestive system (and the assimilation of nutrients), stomach, liver, spleen, gall bladder, and the nervous system. The endocrine gland is also linked to this centre.

Related crystals: citrine, amber, tiger's eye, and yellow calcite.

When in harmony, you have control over emotions and thoughts, as well as a feeling of wholeness, inner calm, and peace. There is a knowing without a doubt, and an acceptance of your place in the universe. You have self-love and, in turn, a great appreciation for all the people in your life and the uniqueness that they bring to the world.

When out of harmony, you feel no or limited trust in the natural flow of life, and doubt and mistrust toward other people. There is a need to control and not truly trust the universe, and you may see blessings as a test. There is an emphasis on the material world and a great need for material security. If any of these elements relate to you, yellow is your healing colour.

Solar Plexus Chakra
Colour: Yellow
10 Petaled Lotus

8.4 Colour Focus: Green

Green relates to the heart chakra located in the centre of the chest. It is the epicentre, or more suitably, the heart of the chakra system. It is my favourite colour and chakra to work with.

It is in this chakra that artistic input (art or music) is transformed into feelings and emotions—where you feel (with the soul, not think with the mind) what you see and hear. An open heart chakra gives you the ability to love freely without fear and self-consciousness. It is the fusion centre of the earthly (body and mind) and the spiritual (soul and heart) elements within ourselves. Negative feelings and emotions (triggered by the mind) are neutralised (by the soul) when one accepts them with an open heart chakra and surrenders in order to purify and cleanse the chaos the mind created.

A fully opened, sparkling-clean heart chakra means that the cheeky friend, the ego, is no longer able to sit in the driver's seat of your life. Feelings of negativity—fear, jealousy, hate, anger, attachment, judgment, resentment—cease to exist within, and so then cease to exist outwardly by way of actions, words, emotions, feelings, thoughts, and perceptions. The key principle is loving beyond the self—basically unconditional love for self and others without attachment, only acceptance. The heart chakra often has a swirl of pink through the green, which is why pink often represents the heart chakra.

Related body parts: heart, upper back, rib cage, chest, skin, lower lungs, circulatory system, and abdominal cavity.

Related crystals: emerald, rose quartz, kunzite, and dioptase.

When in harmony, you experience a feeling of wholeness, inner calm, and peace. Love is pure. There is an acceptance of others, with an ability to empathise—to acknowledge other people's perspectives without any need to understand with the mind or to integrate these perspectives into your own belief system. The concept is, "You are you, I am me—different but one with the same source." Altruism is the purest level of a harmonious heart charka.

When out of harmony, you may give love but not freely, and rewards for imparting love are driven by a lack of self-love and self-confidence. A closed heart chakra makes you unable to accept love given by others because love-for-self is not accepted. Judgments from outside sources (people or events) take precedence over any introspection. Disconnected from your spiritual element and only operating on the earthly element, you rely only on what you see, not what you feel. (I will add that the out-of-harmony characteristics are mostly learnt during childhood and adulthood, and are not a part of your authentic self.) If any of these elements relate to you, green is your healing colour.

Something extra to think about with the heart chakra: When we are born and grow into young beings, we have an open heart chakra, and that explains all the affection, kisses, and cuddles that young beings give without fear or self-consciousness. Heart chakras close or become out of harmony as we grow and are taught the ways of family, community, and society—which is called *family-of-origin imprints*—and how we process our life experiences (self-healing). Knowing this, nurture your children to keep their heart chakras open and teach them self-acceptance, self-belief, and self-confidence. These will establish and fortify their personal physical, emotional, mental, and spiritual boundaries. It's these boundaries that will protect their hearts—as opposed to closing their heart chakra in order to protect their heart. Most healing in our adult years is about clearing and unlearning fear or what does not serve us and returning to love—our authentic self.

Heart Chakra
Colour: Green
12 Petaled Lotus

8.5 Colour Focus: Blue

Blue relates to the throat chakra located at the base of the throat. It governs the aspects of expressing and receiving as the unity between the physical world and spirit. It is the centre where feelings and emotions are transformed into expressions.

Metaphorically, the throat chakra represents people's relationship to their space and the life movie that is playing around them, representing the matrix on which physical reality manifests. An open throat chakra provides for balance in expression—knowing when to be silent and when to speak and express yourself freely and confidently without fear and self-consciousness. The spoken word is the point of creation— the point of manifestation by intent. Words carry energy, and the throat chakra transforms thoughts and feelings into words, creating an energy form via sound.

Related body parts: lungs, vocal cords, throat, thyroid, voice, jaw, and neck.

Related crystals: aquamarine, lapis lazuli and turquoise.

When in harmony, you experience freedom of expression, whether it is silence or speech. Words spoken carry an empowered but compassionate energy. There is an ability to state boundaries and speak up when boundaries have been overstepped, and to restore universal order to a situation. You have the confidence to speak truth and the ability to be silent when others speak of untruth—to determine what should be spoken and what should remain unspoken, and to allow the truth to be learned via the individual's direct life experience.

When out of harmony, you feel a lack of confidence in expressing your truth. Burdened by the opinion of others, you put those opinions first and discount the right to your own truth. Afraid of silence, you fill it with anything including untruth; both sides of expression are stifled. If any of these elements relate to you, blue is your healing colour.

Throat Chakra
Colour: Blue
16 Petaled Lotus

8.6 Colour Focus: Indigo

Indigo relates to the third-eye chakra (also known as the brow chakra) located between the eyes. It governs the aspects of your being and connects to the part of creation that is beyond the physical and science. The third-eye chakra is the gateway to knowing that wisdom is passed down and in turn affects all areas of life. The third-eye chakra is the centre of knowing and the ability to decipher the mental and emotional unbalances within oneself. The third-eye chakra is the power centre of intent and manifestation. It represents all of the elements.

Related body parts: face, eyes, nose, sinus, pituitary gland, and cerebellum.

Related crystals: sodalite, opal, and lapis lazuli.

When in harmony, you are aware of your spiritual side and trust in your own intuition in everyday matters. Intuitive sensitivity becomes the normal way of living, as you acknowledge and foster a constant connection to the universe. The first step to understanding life is intuition; even when the logical mind doesn't have a rational understanding of the information and guidance, there is an inner understanding and sense of harmony.

When out of harmony, you can only see the surface meaning of life; your intuition is blocked. Reactive to mental and emotional pain, you may take on other people's energy unknowingly. You reject being a spiritual being out of a lack of understanding of the intuitive sense, discounting it because of lack of proof via science or logic. You may be even afraid of intuition. If any of these elements relate to you, indigo is your healing colour.

Third Eye Chakra
Colour: Indigo
96 Petaled Lotus

8.7 Colour Focus: Violet (Gold and White)

Violet (gold and white) relates to the crown chakra and is on the top and centre of the head. It is this chakra that connects with the universe through the spiritual self. It is the totality of an individual connecting the physical, mental, emotional, and spiritual aspects of self and offering these to the divine forces of the universe. You express knowledge beyond words and intellect. The crown chakra is the pathway of pure consciousness—the action centre of intent and manifestation.

Related body parts: brain, cerebellum, and skull.

Related crystals: amethyst, clear quartz, alexandrite, and sugilite.

When in harmony, you live with a knowledge of unity, and your self reflects the divine. The ego self is abandoned in favour of the universal self. You take responsibility for negative energy; understand your physical, mental, and emotional bodies; and accept that what you believe, you become—knowing that any expressions of fear or judgement are illusions of the ego. You choose instead to accept all life and acknowledge that individuals are on their soul journey.

When out of harmony, you are unable to let go of anxiety and fear. Unable to imagine the concept of universal unity, you feel depressed and unsatisfied. A major block in the area of soul development greatly limits your ability to heal and recalibrate discord in the physical, mental, and emotional self. If any of these elements relate to you, violet/gold/white is your healing colour.

**Crown Chakra
Colour: Violet, White, Gold
1000 Petaled Lotus**

CHAPTER 9

Plants and Flowers

A great way to spruce up your energy at work or in your home is to introduce living plants. Living plants have a direct connection to Mother Earth's energy grid and provide grounding and flowing energy in your environment. Just keep in mind that our beautiful furry friends—especially our beloved felines—like to play with plants, so make sure that the plants are animal-safe and non-toxic if your pets decide to take a nibble.

Plants will create growth and renew energy in your area. Just make sure you keep them hydrated and alive. If you have trouble remembering to water them, purchase a self-watering pot or place a reminder in your diary to water regularly.

Plants connect us back to nature by sight and then feeling. In addition, plants allow oxygen to increase, which is a biological necessity for our bodies to be healthful.

Flowers are always beautiful in your environment. Again, make sure you keep them in good form and dispose of or replace them when need be to keep positive and clean energy flowing.

The fragrance and constitution of flowers is connected to essential oils, incense, and flower essences and also have spiritual significance in our lives. They are able to transport us through space and time just by sight and smell.

In your selection of flowers, be sure to choose positive-smelling blooms, so that the fragrance will activate positivity in you and your senses. Jasmine, for example, takes me to summer days and warm balmy nights where life is beautiful; I only need to smell the sweet scent to be transported. I often smell jasmine before I see it, so I am sent on a hunt to find the plant that created the beautiful scent that enveloped all my senses.

The same occurs when I smell freshly mowed grass. It reminds me of a spring or summer Sunday at mid-morning, when the sky is blue and the sun is shining and life is all good. This relates to my happy memories of childhood.

The same can be said of perfume; it will activate a memory within you. Just be mindful to activate those positive memories and reminisce over them with gratitude and a smile.

CHAPTER 10

Aroma and Atmosphere

The troposphere is the lowest layer of Mother Earth's atmosphere. It extends from Earth's surface to a height of approximately twelve kilometres. We contribute to the electrical charge in the air surrounding us by how we live. One method of positively infusing the atmosphere around ourselves is with aroma. Below are some ways to use aroma to activate light and harmony in your atmosphere.

10.1 Fresh Air

Fresh air is one of the most refreshing ways to ramp up positivity. You may think fresh air does not have a scent, but consider this example: When you haven't opened a window in a room for some time, a damp, stagnant smell settles in. By opening a window, you allow that damp and stagnant smell to leave your room, allowing fresh air and its scent back in.

Then there is the smell of rain. We all know what rain smells like, and I have never heard anyone claim to dislike the smell. If you can do so without allowing rain to drop on your internal floors and fixtures, open a window or door to let the rain scent into your home. This will increase negative ions (because of the storm clouds) in your space and positive energy along with it.

10.2 Essential Oils

Essential oils are a great way to uplift your environment. Depending on the oils you use, they will welcome in healing energies by a number of methods. I will focus here on the sense of smell.

Typically, essential oils are distilled—with the oil extracted from flowers, leaves, wood, bark, roots, seeds, or peel, depending on the plant. Essential oils are classified depending on their therapeutic properties.

Air fresheners are great also, though keep in mind that they can congest and irritate us as well as our animal friends, producing allergies and sensitivities. Most air fresheners purchased from the supermarket are made of synthetic ingredients. I personally avoid using them, opting for a homemade essential-oil spray or burning incense or oil.

You can use homemade air fresheners that have been made with oils. Make sure, though, that the essential oils are 100 per cent pure; sometimes oils are labelled as *fragrant oils*, and that is an indication that they may be all or partially synthetic. Here is my recipe for an air freshener:

- 200 millilitres captured rain water
- 1/8 teaspoon Himalayan salt (finely ground)
- 16 drops lavender essential oil
- 8 drops orange essential oil
- 4 drops lemon essential oil

- 8 drops patchouli essential oil
- 8 drops frankincense essential oil

Directions:

1. Boil a small amount of the water and pour into a heatproof glass.
2. Add the salt and stir until dissolved.
3. Allow to cool. Pour the salt solution into a glass spray bottle (opaque is best to minimise oxidation of the oils). Add the remainder of the water and then the essential oils.
4. Screw the lid on the bottle and give it a vigorous shake.

Shake the bottle each time before dispersing into the air. I sometimes add a small amethyst or a black tourmaline crystal to the bottle to supercharge the freshener.

Essential oils and their energetic associations are as follows:

- *Frankincense* may be considered the most spiritual incense, as it was given as a gift when Jesus was born, along with myrrh and gold. The traditional telling of the Christmas story includes a key moment where the three wise men from the East arrive and present the Christ child with gifts of gold, frankincense, and myrrh. Frankincense is a purifying and cleansing essential oil, providing energetic protection from discordant energies. It breaks up any energetic imprint of limitation to clear pathways to the divine—to All-That-Is, via your own soul connection during meditation and prayer. It's a majestic oil to use in your sacred space. (Associated chakra: crown)

- *Patchouli* is an essential oil that brings about action—the mantra being "I AM positive change." It has the ability to liberate and activate the limitlessness of life's potential, and to help you see vibrational patterns that colour your life—whether physical, emotional, or mental—and correct them or unlearn what is no longer for your higher good. Patchouli is for remaining alert, as it infuses your life force and inspires you to take action to bring about long-lasting change. It's a perfect oil to use when you move into a new home. (Associated chakra: third eye)

- *Jasmine* eases the highs and lows of your emotions, and therefore has the ability to calm. It assists in endeavours involving love, compassion, and our life purpose. It finds the comparable vibration between the conscious mind and the desires of the heart and welcomes forth angelic realms. It is a fragrance of pure-heart beings. Jasmine is linked with the Goddess Vishnu. It is a divine oil to use in your bedroom. (Associated chakra: third eye)

- *Basil* comes from the Greek *basileus*, meaning "king," as it has come to be associated with the Feast of the Cross commemorating the finding of the True Cross by St. Helena, mother of the emperor Constantine I. Basil has a strong, spicy aroma that is invigorating to the spirit, activating a sense of balance and mental clarity. It is best used when you require a boost of spiritual strength—perhaps the strength of royalty. Basil is ideal for your home office or study. (Associated chakra: third eye)

- *Sage* cleanses and purifies. It helps you tap into esoteric wisdom through your heart and call forth God or All-That-Is and the celestial beings to defend, heal, and protect the human spirit. Sage helps when you find it difficult to understand humanity's actions; it calls in the spiritual energy of divine love. Sage promotes grounding to Mother Earth energies and promotes perseverance of the spirit. It can be used to connect to the energy imprint of your home and purify the environment. Use in all areas of your home. (Associated chakras: third eye and throat)

- *Lavender* originally stems from the Latin word *lavare*, meaning "to wash." Lavender is a calming and relaxing scent, bringing harmony to the soul. It alleviates dense emotional energy, activating decisiveness and emotional balance. Lavender may also be useful for treating anxiety, insomnia, depression, and restlessness. Lavender's relaxedness is great for the living room or bedroom. (Associated chakra: throat)

- *Neroli* brings peace to the soul. It extends up to your higher self and your spiritual existence, especially when you have temporarily lost your connection to your higher self. Neroli helps you heal and brings light and joy in and around you. It can help repair rifts or arguments that stem from disconnections of the spirit. Neroli's peacefulness and gentleness make it great for the bedroom. (Associated chakra: throat)

- *Rose* is the aroma of the contentment and happiness of heart energy. It is the aroma for patience—whether you require this energy to manifest it or intend to magnify it. Rose allows these energies to amplify, allowing one to experience gratitude. The seventeenth-century

English physician Culpeper wrote that red roses strengthen the heart. He may have been referring to a physical action, but inhaling the aroma of fresh roses—which is an automatic reaction when roses are in the vicinity—strengthens the heart spiritually and emotionally. Culpeper attributed many other healing properties to the rose, from cooling to astringent benefits. Rose can be used in any room of your home. (Associated chakra: heart)

- *Geranium* has a loving, balancing, and uplifting effect. It has the ability to break down fear and feelings of abandonment, whether from childhood or adulthood. It is an aroma of love and commitment, balancing the male and female energies within and around you. It brings joy to your space and energy field, and it deflects lower vibrational energies. It's a beautiful oil to use in your bedroom. (Associated chakra: heart)

- *Ylang ylang* encourages self-confidence and shields your soul and spirit from negative influences. For those with troubled minds, ylang ylang is calming and soothing. If you find it difficult to embody self-love, to forgive yourself, or to find a place in your heart to allow forgiveness to come in, ylang ylang is perfect for you. It aids you in acknowledging our wonderful world and the life you are experiencing, and it allows you to notice, with love and understanding that we are all connected and experiencing life at the same time, albeit with different life purposes. The forgiving energy of ylang ylang is perfect for a meditation room or sacred space. (Associated chakra: solar plexus)

- *Lemon* is a native of India. The name is derived from the Arabic *laimun* or the Persian *limu*, which is a cognate of a Sanskrit word meaning "lime." Lemon is cleansing to spiritual bodies as well as the physical body, and it helps release patterning to bring about joy and hopefulness with clear thought and then feeling. Lemon's cleansing nature makes it perfect for the bathroom. (Associated chakra: solar plexus)

- *Sandalwood*, in many cultures and religions of the world, occupies a place of dignity and respect—especially in the Hindu religion, where it is considered holy and essential. It is offered to the various Hindu gods and goddesses. Sandalwood encourages a meditative state that helps you link your physical self to your spiritual self. It brings unity to help you connect harmoniously with humanity. More than that, it provides spiritual protection to all levels of the spiritual body. This spiritually meaningful aroma is divinely ideal for use in a meditation room or sacred space. (Associated chakra: sacral)

- *Orange* brings happiness to the heart, regeneration to the spirit, and vitality to the soul. The fresh and stimulating scent inspires insight, promotes light-heartedness, and activates creativity of the soul. Orange conquers fears and obsessions. The creative aroma is best-suited for use in your lounge room. (Associated chakra: sacral)

- *Myrrh* was given as a gift when Jesus was born, along with frankincense and gold. It is associated with acceptance, calm, and peace. Spiritually, myrrh links with the pathway of the soul, where we have many life paths to choose from. Myrrh helps you to let go, to forgive, and to move forward on your chosen path. It calms and anchors peace to the body, mind, and soul. Myrrh is perfect for your meditation room, sacred space, and living room. (Associated chakra: base)

- *Peppermint* has long been known for its medicinal value; its impressively long history often gives it the prestigious title of the world's oldest medicine. Peppermint is strong and clearing, with a vibrant energy that raises awareness of self and the universe, activating your sensitivity to recognise wisdom in other realms. Peppermint stimulates and uplifts, promoting regeneration and concentration. It may be used to clear a pathway. The regeneration of peppermint is great for your home office, kitchen, and bedroom, as appropriate. (Associated chakras: base, sacral, solar plexus, and throat)

10.3 Candles

Candles are a lovely way to incorporate aroma and light into your environment. The first candles are said to have been developed by the ancient Egyptians. They were used for many years to provide light at night, for night travels and during religious ceremonies. In almost all Hindu homes, candles are lit daily before the altar of the Lord. Candles are a traditional part of Buddhist ritual observances, and they are used in Sikhism on Diwali, the festival of light.

Candles are used in most churches and placed at altars with significance. In Christianity, the three elements of a lit altar candle symbolise Jesus Christ: the beeswax or other wax material symbolising his body, the wick his soul, and the flame his divinity. When people pass over, we tend to light candles for them, symbolising their soul and signifying that it is of light and eternal. The symbolism of prayer has been connected with candles, with the burning flame representing the prayer that rises to God or All-That-Is.

In light of this, candles are used with intention of positive manifestation of peace, prosperity, and abundance, being in direct connection to God or All-That-Is. Candles of different colours can be utilised to heal or strengthen the chakras, as covered in the previous chapter. It is up to you, and intuition plays a part in this.

I tend to use candles when I meditate or say my prayers. The soft, divine energy they emanate is very relaxing.

10.4 Incense

Incense has been used for many years in many sacred processes. When we introduce elements into our home environment, we also welcome the associated energy to the imprint and the intention that we set when we do.

I burn frankincense and myrrh often in my home, with the intent of clearing any stagnant, discordant, or mis-qualified energy that may have entered my home. As I mentioned, frankincense and myrrh were given as gifts when Jesus was born, along with gold. Both hold great spiritual significance and purifying energy.

You can purchase incense sticks to burn, which come in a range of beautiful scents. Nag champa incense has a magical, powdery floral fragrance. The champa flower is the spiritual scent of India and is used primarily for meditation and used in sacred spaces.

You can also purchase incense sticks in the scents discussed in Section 10.2 on essential oils. They will have the same spiritual significance.

CHAPTER 11

Sound

In physics, sound is a vibration that transmits as a wave of pressure and movement through a medium like air or water. In physiology and psychology, sound is the reception of such waves and the response by the brain. The brain interprets the sound and signals a response in the body. If the response is one of peace and calm, that aligns your body to a state that matches your soul vibration. That's where you can align the mind, body, and soul in frequency.

Sound can have an incredible healing affect. We tend to pay most attention to our sense of sight, and unfortunately, we don't fully utilise our senses of smell, taste, and sound. I constantly have my favourite meditation music playing in the background in my home. While it is on low volume, it still fills my home with peace and tranquillity. It suits me, as I don't watch TV often, and it keeps my space in a relaxed and serene state.

I am not suggesting that you cease watching TV—just don't discount the impact that sound has on you and your energy field. The healing and stabilising benefits of playing meditation music in the background are remarkable. It doesn't have to be meditation music, either. It can be jazz or relaxing music or even the sounds of the ocean or our beautiful whale and dolphin friends—anything that brings a feeling of peace and tranquillity via sound waves to impact your vibration.

Wind chimes will bring the same vibrations to your environment and energy field as well. Bamboo and metal produce different frequencies, but both are still tranquil. Bells can also break up and disperse energy that may be stagnant. They are often used to clear sacred spaces and cleanse crystals, as well as break any interfering energy that is present. Many Christian Churches ring bells in a church tower, which I find is a "joyful sound," as it reminds me of God's presence in the world.

Crystal singing bowls may just be the most beautiful sound. I often bring these bowls out when I have visitors, and the "music" they play is of the heavens. The tones produced by crystal singing bowls are heard by your ears and felt in your body and chakras. The bowls come in difference sizes and hence carry different frequencies. Crystal singing bowls are perfect for clearing, healing, balancing, and enhancing meditation.

Tibetan singing bowls are said to date back to the time of Buddha Shakyamuni (560–480 BC). The tradition was brought from India to Tibet, along with the teachings of the Buddha, by the great tantric master Padmasambhava in the eighth century AD.

Tibetan singing bowls produce sounds that invoke a deep state of relaxation, which helps us to enter into meditation. Again, they come in different sizes, so the frequency they amplify varies. They can be found in temples and monasteries throughout the world.

I mentioned before that we tend focus on our sense of sight and forget the impact of the sense of sound. Yet it is just as important as our sense of sight in terms of activation of feelings and emotions. Here is an example of how sound impacts our energy field: When you hear a song start to play on the radio, in a store or at a social function, you may be reminded of a happy or sad time in your life. That song—in the present moment, via the sense of sound—activates feelings, emotions, and memories within you that you experienced in the past. As such, the song takes you from the present moment into your past. That is how sound impacts our energy field. Utilise the sense of sound to positively impact your energy field.

Tibetan Singing Bowl

CHAPTER 12

Sacred Geometry and Symbology

Sacred geometry and symbology have been used for thousands of centuries, and they are commonly used in today's society. We associate geometric shapes, patterns, or symbols with circumstances and conditions on our roads to prepare us for what lies ahead. We connect to these shapes and symbols, and they influence us on many levels.

Sacred geometry is the historical significance of a shape, pattern, or form. Symbology is what an individual associates with a pattern or shape from his or her current understanding. Stars, for example, have many positive connotations. An upright cross or star carries divine energy embodied in a physical form. The infinity symbol reminds us that nothing has a start or an end; the ego attributes a start and an end on a physical level, but on a spiritual level, everything is infinite, limitless and omnipresent.

Symbols are also used for healing. Reiki is a healing modality where universal life force is activated, by way of symbolically motioning the dominate hand to bring about universal life force energy to energise and heal people, spaces, and situations.

The power of sacred geometry and symbols lies in the intent of the use and also in an individual's knowledge of the symbols' use in history. Sometimes you will have two perceptions of its use and meaning. Go with whatever is intuitively right for you and what you find resonates with you and your soul.

12.1 Cross

The cross is a symbol representing Jesus Christ and the faith of Christians. The cross is the central symbol of the Christian religion, as it signifies the crucifixion of Jesus Christ—referred to as the Passion—and Jesus's redemptive death, which concerns the doctrines of salvation and atonement. Today, the cross is a symbol of the resurrection of Jesus Christ, the victory over sin and death, and eternal life.

12.2 Om

Om, pronounced *aum*, is a Sanskrit word and a sacred sound. The om symbol is a spiritual symbol in Indian belief.

Om is an important symbol and mantra in Hinduism, Buddhism, and Jainism. It is found in ancient monasteries and temples, and it is contained within spiritual manuscripts, such as at the beginning and end of chapters in the Vedas. The Vedas are among the oldest sacred texts and are said to date from 1700–1100 BC. The symbol is also found within the Upanishads and Yoga Sūtras of Patañjali.

Om is representative of the soul, the higher self, the God within—in unity with the universe, truth, omnipresent energy, divine love, and holy knowledge.

12.3 Infinity

The infinity symbol ∞ (sometimes called the lemniscate) was originally a mathematical symbol representing the concept of infinity, introduced with its mathematical meaning in 1655. In today's age, the infinity symbol is frequently used to represent infinite life, love, faith, and protection. You will find it on many items, including paintings, jewellery, and even used as tattoos. Once again, the power is in the intent of the use of the infinity symbol. Most people will recognise it as a representation of the soul as infinite rather than a mathematical sign.

12.4 Circle

The word *circle* is derived from the Greek word *kirkos* or *kuklos*, meaning "hoop" or "ring." The circle has been known since before the beginning of recorded history. Natural circles would have been observed, such as the moon and sun. Ancient Greek philosopher and mathematician Plato (428–347 BC) refers to circles in the seventh letter, describing them as "round" and "annular." They might be defined as that which has an equal distance from its circumference to its centre everywhere.

A circle signifies continuity, balance, and equality. The circle is the only shape used to compose the Flower of Life.

12.5 Peace

The olive branch as a symbol of peace in Western civilisation dates at least to the fifth century BC. The olive tree symbolized plenty, but the ancient Greeks believed that it also drove away evil spirits. The story of Noah in the Bible ends with a passage describing a dove bringing a freshly plucked olive leaf, a sign of life after the flood and of God's bringing Noah, his family, and the animals to land.

The dove and olive branch were used to represent peace symbolically by early Christians, and then eventually became a secular peace symbol, popularised by Pablo Picasso after the Second World War. In the 1950s, the "peace sign," as it is known today, was designed as the logo for the British Campaign for Nuclear Disarmament and adopted by anti-war and counterculture activists in the United States and elsewhere. The V hand signal and the peace flag also became international peace symbols. The sign is now used all around the world for many causes to signify anti-war and world peace.

12.6 Classical Elements

Plato seems to have been the first to use the term *element* in reference to air, fire, earth, and water. Aristotle (384–322 BC), a Greek philosopher and scientist, later related each of the four elements to two of the four sensible qualities. Aristotelian elements and qualities are hot, dry, wet, and cold.

1. *Air* is the first of the four classical elements in ancient Greek philosophy and science. It is often seen as a universal power or pure substance. Its supposed fundamental importance to life can be seen in words like *aspire*, *inspire*, *perspire*, and *spirit*, all derived from the Latin *spirare*. According to Plato, air is associated with the *octahedron*. Aristotle considered air to be primarily hot and secondarily wet. The alchemical symbol for air is an upward-pointing triangle bisected by a horizontal line.

2. *Fire* is the second of the four classical elements. It has been commonly associated with the qualities of energy, assertiveness, and passion. In one Greek myth, Prometheus stole fire from the gods to protect otherwise helpless humans, but he was punished for this charity. According to Plato, fire is associated with the *tetrahedron*. Aristotle considered fire to be primarily hot and secondarily dry. The alchemical symbol for fire is an upward-pointing triangle.

3. *Water* is the third of the elements in ancient Greek philosophy and science, in the Asian Indian system Panchamahabhuta, and in the Chinese cosmological and physiological system Wu Xing. In contemporary esoteric traditions, it is commonly associated with the qualities of emotion and intuition. According to

Plato, water is associated with the *icosahedron*. Aristotle considered water to be primarily cold and secondarily wet. The alchemical symbol for water is a downward-pointing triangle.

4. Earth is the fourth of the four classical elements. It was commonly associated with qualities of heaviness, matter, and the terrestrial world. According to Plato, earth is associated with the *cube* or *hexahedron*. Aristotle considered earth primarily cold and secondarily dry. The alchemical symbol for earth is a downward-pointing triangle bisected by a horizontal line.

Here is something to consider: if you bring together, centre, and overlap all four elements—air, fire, water and earth—they will form a hexagram, also known as the Star of David.

The Classical Elements

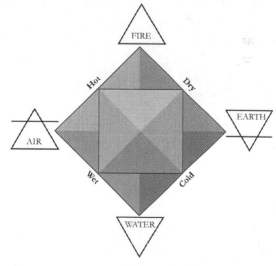

12.7 Ether

There is no defined symbol for ether from Plato's time, as he did not define it in the classical elements. Aristotle did add a fifth element of ether, known as the quintessence. The reasoning was that fire, earth, air, and water were earthly and corruptible; spirit, the purest, was composed of heavenly or celestial bodies.

Quintessence (after *quint* meaning "fifth," and *quinta essentia* in French, from medieval Latin) is called *aether* in ancient Greece and *akasha* in India. Akasha ("space" in Sanskrit) is the all-pervading ether in which records of past events are imprinted.

The concept of the five elements is referenced in both Hinduism and Buddhism. In esoteric Hinduism, the four elements describe matter, and a fifth element describes that which is beyond the material and physical world. Analogous concepts existed in ancient China and Japan. In the modern world, ether is often symbolised by the wheel of life, similar to the Buddhist wheel of dharma, recognised as a circle outlining eight octants.

12.8 Wheel of Life

In Buddhist symbology, the wheel of life (also referred to as the wheel of dharma and the wheel of laws) symbolises the cycle of life, death, and rebirth. The hub represents the discipline of meditation. The eight octants refer to Buddha's teachings about the eightfold path of life to reach nirvana.

12.9 Flower of Life

The Flower of Life is the name given to a geometric figure composed of multiple evenly spaced, overlapping circles. This figure forms a flower-like pattern with the symmetrical structure of a hexagon. A Flower of Life symbol consists of seven or more overlapping circles, in which the centre of each circle is on the circumference of up to six surrounding circles of the same diameter.

The Flower of Life is said to date back a couple thousand years and is considered to provide deep spiritual meaning and forms of enlightenment to those who have studied it as sacred geometry. One phenomenal, and not well understood, ancient structure in Egypt is the Osirion, which is located at Abydos. The Osirion is situated behind and underneath the Temple of Seti I. Flower of Life symbols were painted with red ochre paint (a natural earth pigment containing hydrated iron oxide, with a large amount of hematite crystal making it red) onto the stone. The other markings, which appear to be letters, are thought to be Greek, which would date the markings to the first century AD.

The Flower of Life signifies that everything and everyone is connected to the one source, and so we are all one of the same. It suggests that the Flower of Life is symbolic of ancient wisdom. Today, it is often used in crystal gridding and in art and jewellery.

The Flower of Life

12.10 Platonic Solids

The five Platonic solids are ideal and primitive structures of crystal patterns that occur throughout the world of minerals. These are the only five regular polyhedral (meaning three-dimensional solids made up of flat and straight surfaces and sharp corners) from the same equilateral, equiangular polygons. (A polygon is a two-dimensional shape made up of straight lines, with all the lines connecting up and leaving no openings in the peripheries.)

Plato is the one most associated with the identification of the following five regular symmetrical three-dimensional shapes, which he maintained were the basis for the whole universe:

1. *Tetrahedron* is the first of the platonic solids. It has four triangular sides and represents the element of fire.

2. *Cube or hexahedron* is the second platonic solid. It has six square sides and represents the element of earth.

3. *Octahedron* is the third of the platonic solids. It has eight triangular sides and represents the element of air.

4. *Icosahedron* is the forth platonic solid. It has twenty triangular sides and represents the element of water.

5. *Dodecahedron* is the fifth and final platonic solid. It has twelve pentagonal sides and represents the universe.

The Platonic Solids

TETRAHEDRON	CUBE OR (HEXAHEDRON)	OCTAHEDRON	ICOSAHEDRON	DODECAHEDRON
4 Sided	*6 Sided*	*8 Sided*	*20 Sided*	*12 Sided*
FIRE △	EARTH ⩊	AIR △	WATER ▽	AETHER ✪
4 Faces	*6 Faces*	*8 Faces*	*20 Faces*	*12 Faces*
4 Points	*8 Points*	*6 Points*	*12 Points*	*20 Points*
6 Edges	*12 Edges*	*12 Edges*	*30 Edges*	*30 Edges*

12.11 Pentagram (Five-Pointed Star)

The pentagram is an upright five-pointed star. It was said to be used in ancient times as a Christian symbol for the five senses or the five wounds of Christ. Christian use of the five-pointed star occurs back many centuries, and was eventually replaced with the cross.

As I said, symbolism is what an individual associates with a shape. Sacred geometry is the historical significance, the energy from where it first originated.

The five-pointed star, in its upright position (one point upward and two points downward), is even depicted the national flags of some countries, such as Ethiopia and Vietnam. There are more than fifty countries with various five-pointed stars on their national flag.

12.12 Star Tetrahedron and Hexagram

The hexagram is a six-pointed star in two-dimensional form, also known as the Star of David or Shield of David. The star tetrahedron, better known as the merkabah, is a six-pointed star in three-dimensional form. Both symbols are featured in Jewish belief systems in which they carry great significance as protection and connection to the divine.

Merkabah in Hebrew means "chariot". Early Jewish mysticism centred on visions found in the Book of Ezekiel relating to the throne-chariot of God, which conveyed Ezekiel into heaven.

In modern times, the star tetrahedron and the hexagram upright (one point pointing up and down, and two points pointing to each side) represent the link and interconnection between heaven and earth, the physical and spiritual. As the saying goes, "As above, so below."

In visualisation, the star tetrahedron encompasses the physical body from head to toe, which aligns with the chakra system and the connection to the divine. Also, the symbols for the classical elements of air, fire, water, and earth from Plato's time combine to make a star tetrahedron, indicating all elements coming together in unity.

The star tetrahedron and the hexagram is said to provide protection and a flowing connection to the divine, God, or All-That-Is.

CHAPTER 13

Your Vehicle

Your vehicle is symbolically an extension of yourself. Your vehicle and its mechanical functioning can serve as an indicator of the workings of your body. If you experience battery problems with your car, ask yourself, how charged and rejuvenated is your own energy? Are you operating on low levels, and if so, what is causing this low level of energy? If your motor is causing you problems, what may be going on in the thoracic region of your body or your heart chakra?

If you do not have a car, this chapter is of little relevance, although you can try applying this concept to your motorbike or bicycle. If you use a bike for transportation, one thing is evident: you have adopted a simpler way of life. If nothing else, you can decipher information for those you know who do drive motor vehicles.

Mechanical reliability is the important factor. Make sure your vehicle is mechanically sound and reliable. When you experience issues with your vehicle, you may be able to decipher the connection this has to your life, much the same way that you can find the spiritual significance of physical ailments and disease, which can be interpreted as corresponding to the blocks within your mental, emotional, and spiritual life. It is an interesting indicator, but utilise this as a guide and helpful hint only and not the be-all and end-all. As with all physical ailments and diseases, consult a qualified medical practitioner when required.

CHAPTER 14

For Healers and Therapists: Treatment Spaces

Healers and therapists can apply each chapter in this book to their treatment spaces or rooms. It is important to acknowledge that other people will be welcomed to participate in their own healing in this space, so it should be representative of this acknowledgment. Treatment spaces should be neutral, protected, and safe spaces connected to source energy, meaning that you as the healer recognise yourself as the vessel who is the channel—and a soul who allows spirit to facilitate healing and expansion for other souls through you.

Your treatment spaces should be protected for both the healer and the healee, nurturing and free from any egoistic interference to the healing process that spirit has assigned to you. The main concept of treatment spaces is the transmutation of negative and discordant energies, whether they have been brought in by the healer or the healed. You can apply the concepts of each chapter in this book as follows:

- location and structure
- crystal gridding
- Himalayan salt to combat electromagnetic smog

- previous residents
- neighbours and the past
- decluttering to remove blocks
- cleanliness to promote clean energy
- cleansing to clear discordant energy
- interior design to improve flow
- colour therapy
- plants and flowers
- aroma and atmosphere
- sound
- sacred geometry and symbology

The final aspect you will need to contemplate is intent. The intent of any treatment spaces of a healer or therapist is "First, do no harm." In Latin, this is *"Primum non nocere,"* which originated from Hippocrates and is known as the Hippocratic Oath. Many practitioners, in particular physicians, swear by this oath. It basically indicates an obligation to treat the ill to the best of one's ability, to preserve a patient's privacy, and to teach the secrets of medicine to the next generation.

Ensure that your treatment spaces reflects this intent. Questions that healers may ask themselves include "What motivates me to be a vessel to help heal?" and "What is it that drives me to provide healing for others— money, a sense of power, a sense of service to the world, compassion?" It is very important for all healers to understand their intentions. Make sure that you first do no harm to the individuals you treat and that your treatment spaces are free of any discord or negative energy, and especially any personal experiences that the healer may be working through.

CHAPTER 15

Conclusion

I hope you have gained wisdom from *How to Create Positive Energy in Your Space*. The concepts that I write about are what I do in my personal spaces, and I share these bits of wisdom so that you can live life without unnecessary interference (energy outside of yourself) and focus on your path of becoming self–realised in this lifetime.

When you are on this spiritual path, you become intuitively sensitive to energy around you, and I truly desire for you to acknowledge and understand this. My hope for you is to be able to easily and instantaneously decipher and intuit the difference between your own energy and the energy outside yourself that you may be sensing. If you cannot determine, by connecting to your heart charka, why you are feeling a type of energy, it is a general indication that it has not been created within you.

To narrow it down, there are four reasons you may encounter negative experiences or situations in your life:

1. You allowed, albeit unknowingly, an external source of negative energy (imprints, opinions, thoughts, or projections) to impact your energy field and life.
2. Your thoughts created the negative energy and it manifested.
3. It was negative karma returning to you to be resolved, from this and past lives.
4. A lesson that is a part of your soul journey needs to be learned and integrated into your way of being, such as self-love and compassion.

When something goes wrong in your life, figure out which one of these it involves and take suitable action to either change it, clear it, heal it, or learn from it.

Explanation number 1 and 2, to a lesser extent, are addressed in *How to Create Positive Energy in Your Space*. If you wish to learn more, my first book Living in Light, Love & Truth, explores all four explanations in depth. I have explained what to do about energy that is not of your creation and the effect of accepting that negative energy as your own and allowing it to impact your thoughts and therefore manifest. If you can practice self-awareness and identify when the negative energy you are sensing is from outside of yourself, there is little chance you will mistakenly assume that it is your energy, so you can save yourself the process of going through the cycle of self healing of negative energy that has not been created by you in the first place. This will leave you more time to invest in yourself and your life path and living the life that spirit so wants you to live.

That said, always practice energetic responsibility toward yourself, others, and all living things. Enjoy the clean, fresh energy you have created in the now positively and divinely protected space you call home. Always remember, the universe doesn't conspire against you—the universe conspires in support of you.

Namaste and God Bless,

Kasi Kaye Iliopoulos

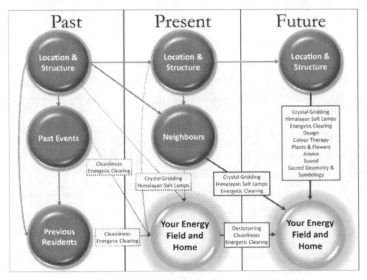

Energetic imprints in your environment and your energy field - this diagram demonstrates the methods and factors that may affect your life, as we explored in How to Create Positive Energy in your Space

Printed in the United States
By Bookmasters